I Want A Pet Parakeet

Gail Forsyth

This publication has been researched and designed to provide accurate pet care, while helping children learn the responsibilities that entail having to care for their pet parakeet.

No part of this book is to be copied without written permission from the publisher and author.

Breed Profiles Publishing
Cedar City, UT 84721

All rights reserved. © 2013

Table of Contents

Note To Parents From The Author	1
Acknowledgment	2
My Pledge	3
Personal Page For Your Parakeet	4
Always Wash Your Hands	5
General Information on Parakeets	6
Door Hanger	9
Questions and Answers	11
Word Find	12
Free Flight	13
My Own Playpen	14
Color Us	15
Draw Me Some Wings	16
My Cage	17
Healthy Foods For Parakeets	19
What Foods Not To Feed Your Parakeet	21
Vitamins & Minerals	22
Questions and Answers on Food	23
Color These Four Parakeets	24
Toys	25
Grooming Your Parakeet	26
My Feathers	27
My Beak	28
Teaching Your Parakeet To Talk	29
Taking Your Parakeet Outdoors	30
Parakeet Maze	31
Color Us	32
Health Issues for Parakeets	33
Missing Vowels	34
Word Find	35
Color Me	36
Daily Care Chart	37
Make Your Own Note Cards	38
Make Your Own Bookmark	41
Other Books in the Series	43

Note To Parents From The Author

As a parent and grandparent myself, I know the cries and wants of a child that desires a pet. When I was a child I had the same wishes to obtain just about every kind of pet I could. Every book I bought or checked out at the library was pet or animal related.

If your child has been asking for a parakeet, only you know if he or she is ready to take on that commitment. Your supervision will ensure that the pet is being well cared for and you'll be pleased with watching your child learn to care and nurture a pet. They may even grow up to follow a career in the pet field.

Parakeets can be a good choice for children. They don't require a lot of care, or any special licenses or tend to bite the mailman.

You'll find this book will help your child learn about the needs of their parakeet and all the while having a fun time doing it. The book has basic care topics that your child can read, plus interactive games, mazes, questions and answers, and care charts.

Childhood lasts such a short time, but the memories with a pet will last a lifetime.

Gail

Acknowledgment

I would like to acknowledge my family for all their help and words of encouragement while taking the idea for the books all the way to getting them published.

To my mother, who certainly endured some trying years when I would bring home every animal I could get my hands on.

To my children, who are a great inspiration in so much of who I am, and whose father inspired them into becoming the fine adults they are today.

To my husband, for his endless patience on the time I've spent with my own pets. It is not true that the pets eat better than he does!

A great big "Thank You" to each and every one of you.

My Pledge

Being a responsible pet owner, I understand that it takes daily care to be sure that my parakeet gets the care it deserves.

I pledge to give my parakeet food and fresh water every day.

I pledge to never abuse my parakeet. I will never hit my parakeet.

I pledge to give my parakeet some out of the cage playtime as often as I can, everyday would be wonderful.

I pledge to keep my parakeet's cage clean.

I pledge to read books on parakeets, if I need to find out something about their care.

I pledge to always wash my hands after playing or cleaning up after my parakeet.

Signed,   Date:

_____   _____

Personal Page For Your Parakeet

Your Name _____

Your Age _____

Parakeet's Name _____

Parakeet's Age _____

Color of Your Parakeet _____

Date Obtained _____

Obtained From _____

Veterinarian _____

Paste a Picture of You and Your

Parakeet Here

**Always Wash Your Hands After Playing or Cleaning Up After Your Parakeet
Draw Some Colorful Bubbles!**

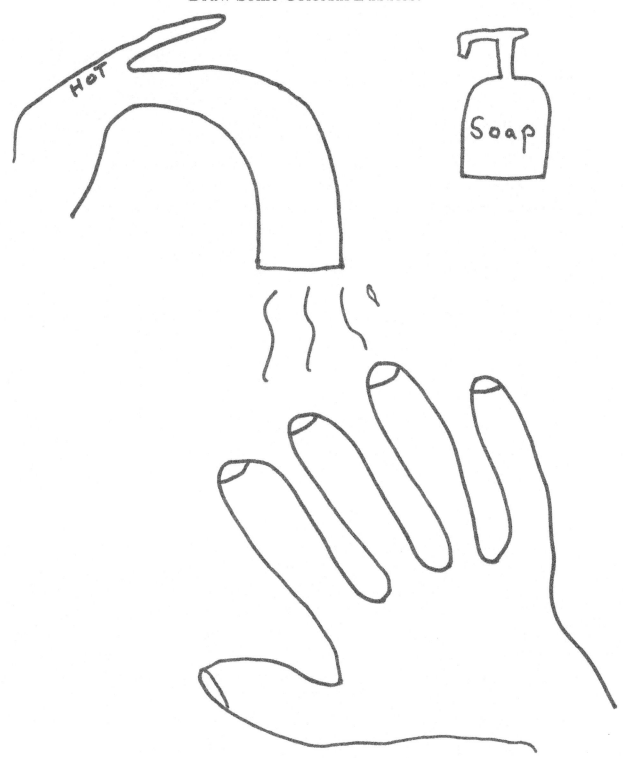

General Information on Parakeets

So, you've been wanting a pet parakeet. You've promised to take care of it, feed it and clean up after it. You think a parakeet would be fun to have as a pet. Well, I am a parakeet and my name is Perky. It takes more than just playing, petting and admiring my good looks to give me the proper care that I need. I'll tell you a little bit about what I like and what you'll need to do to make me happy and keep me healthy.

All in all, I am pretty easy to take care of. Just remember that all my care will fall on your shoulders. I can't get my own water, my own food or adjust the temperature to keep me comfortable. I also need daily exercise and interaction with you. My care will have to last my whole life, each and everyday, not just for a few weeks. Are you willing to do this for me? If your answer is yes, then this book will help you to learn how to take care of me.

Here is some general information on pet parakeets. We'll discuss some of these topics in a little more depth, throughout the book.

I am a clean creature and I like a clean home.

I am a bird.

I have wings so I can fly.

My average life span is between 5 and 10 years, sometimes longer.

Did you know that I do not have teeth?

I need to chew things to keep my beak worn down.

I come in lots of different colors.

I will grow to about 9 inches long, from the top of my head to my tail.

I only weigh about 1 and ½ ounces. I am really small and delicate.

Parakeets can be very affectionate.

I am a social creature and very friendly once I am tamed.

Parakeets are easy to tame. I must be handled often to stay tame. I must learn to trust you and be assured that you will not harm me. Start slowly to pet and stroke my chest and my back. Give me a tasty treat while doing this.

As I get more relaxed you can try to get me on your finger, by gently pushing your finger against my chest. Doing this will make me step onto your finger. Practice this while I am in my cage. I may fly away from you at first.

Don't move too fast around me and don't make loud noises. These will really scare me. Once you get me on your finger don't spin me in circles. Don't throw me up in the air. Never, ever hit me. Even a slight tap can hurt or possibly kill me. I won't forget if you have hurt me and this will make me scared of you.

I don't usually bite for no reason, once I am tame. I may try to bite if I am scared. Be sure my treats are big enough so that I don't accidentally nip your fingers while you are holding them. Don't tease me or bang on my cage if I am making noise. It's just me, being a parakeet and doing what parakeets do.

Go slow and be patient with me if I seem scared or skittish. Always let me see you coming to get me. Don't swoop down too fast, or I'll fuss and bite to try to get away. Talk to me gently. Before long, I'll eagerly await your visits and look forward to our time together. We'll be best friends.

We are intelligent creatures and training me to do tricks will depend on how much time you spend with me.

If there is one trick to teach me it would be to have me come to you by ringing a bell. Then if I ever get lost or if you need to put me back in my cage quickly, just a ring of the bell will bring me flying and I'll be looking for a treat. Practice this everyday. Ring the bell and offer me the treat. Don't expect me to learn this overnight. But soon, one day I just might surprise you.

Be sure that the house or room I fly in is bird proofed for my safety. Cover glass windows and mirrors so I don't fly into them. Be sure any open water containers are covered, such as an aquarium, bathtub or sink. It is best not to let me fly in the kitchen, especially when the stove is being used. Or if someone is doing any cooking. Any hot liquid or foods are very dangerous for me. The garbage disposal is also very dangerous when it is turned on.

Parakeets are curious creatures.

My cage of course, can keep me safe from other animals when I am locked up in it. Once I'm out of the cage and exploring, be sure that any other animals are locked up in another room so that they don't hurt me. One pounce from a cat or dog can do me great harm.

Some dogs and cats may accept me into the household. I may jump when the dog or cat comes closer to me and that may trigger the natural instinct in cats and many dogs to try to catch me. Some may think that they are only playing with me. I'm small and delicate and should not play with dogs or cats.

Never trust the cat around me. Just having the cat constantly watching me can make me nervous.

While I'm flying around outside my cage, be extra cautious that nobody opens the door that leads out of the house. I might fly outside. You can hang a little sign on the door that says, "Parakeet is Loose" to warn them that I am out of my cage.

The next page has a handy door hanger for you to color, cut out and hang on your door. Decorate the back side of the door hanger too.

Door Hanger

Color this door hanger, cut it out and hang it on the door when I am allowed to have some free time out of my cage.

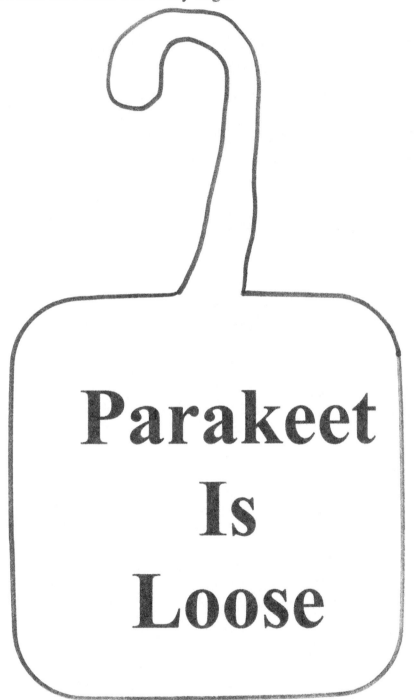

Make A Backside of the Door Hanger

parakeets are Loose

Questions and Answers

Here are six questions for you to answer on my basic housing and care. You will find all the answers in the previous section on General Information on Parakeets. Read it as many times as you like.

How long do parakeets normally live? _____

Can I sleep with the cat? _____

Do I have teeth? _____

Will I rub my beak to keep it worn down? _____

Can I learn to talk? _____

Is a mirror fun for me to have? _____

I hope you got all the answers correct.

Word Find

Below is a word find puzzle. These words all pertain to parakeets, and you can find them in the section called General Information on Parakeets. Circle the words and check them off the list when you find them.

___ CLEAN

___ PARAKEET

___ ACTIVE

___ CURIOUS

___ PLAYFUL

___ SOCIAL

___ CLIMB

___ FLY

___ BEAK

___ TAME

C	T	P	A	R	A	K	E	E	T	E	G	U	I	N	N	M	O
U	A	F	R	E	Q	E	A	R	S	K	S	O	C	I	A	L	O
R	M	F	A	C	T	I	V	E	O	R	E	F	R	A	T	S	P
I	E	R	M	G	I	C	D	O	P	C	U	R	I	O	U	S	U
P	J	I	S	Y	T	L	F	D	V	B	S	A	R	G	U	O	N
P	I	H	W	Q	S	I	A	C	D	G	C	L	I	M	B	S	J
I	U	G	U	I	N	M	A	P	I	G	J	W	F	A	Z	X	X
G	M	T	M	V	K	B	J	Q	W	R	O	D	E	N	T	T	Y
G	P	L	A	Y	F	U	L	A	N	W	C	L	E	V	E	R	W
S	B	E	A	K	S	B	C	A	X	S	Z	O	A	Y	F	L	Y

Free Flight

Letting your parakeet have free flight in your house is something that you and the rest of your family will have to decide on.

First off, yes I would enjoy it. Birds were meant to fly.

However, free flight also can come with many dangers. The first of course is that I might fly right out the door or an open window.

The best place for me to have some free flight is in only one room at a time and under your supervision. You should be able to close all windows and doors in this room. Put the door hanger that you colored and cut out, on the outside of the door, to let others know that I am on the loose. This way they won't let the cat in or me out.

Only let me fly freely if you can stay with me the whole time and keep an eye on me. When you have to do other things, simply put me back in my cage. This will keep me safe.

If I seem to perch up high, like on the top of the window or door frames, start to teach me to get on a long stick, shaped like a perch. Then you can put the stick up to me, while I am on the window or door frame and urge me to get on it. Give me a treat each time. This will take some practice but will be worth it when you want me back in my cage.

If you decide not to give me free flight, a very large cage will help me spread my wings and get in some flight time.

Either way I'll be happy if you spend some time with me everyday.

My Own Playpen

Having my own playpen or yard would be a special treat to go to each day.

You could even make me a special place right on a fold out card table.

Be sure to put some paper down on the card table. Especially under any perches or swings.

Then just add some toys for me to climb on. Ladders, perches, swings, and even some small sturdy boxes.

This might be a good place for me to take a bath too, when it is time.

Add a mirror.

Switch my toys around. This keeps things fun and stimulating for me.

Now let your imagination begin. Hide a small treat for me under a little toy. I have a good sense of smell and with your help, I'll soon toss the toy aside to get at the treat.

Teach me how to ring a little bell. Hold a treat next to the bell, as I reach for the treat, the bell will ring and of course, you'll give me the treat as my reward.

You'll want to be sure that I am tamed down before trying to introduce me to the playpen. Once I realize how much fun the playpen is, I'll look forward to these outings with you each and every day.

When my playtime is over, clean up the paper and any messes that I've made so that the next time it is all clean and ready for me to play on.

Besides good exercise for me, these outings will make you laugh at my antics and will keep me from getting bored in my regular cage and make me so glad that I am your parakeet.

Color Us

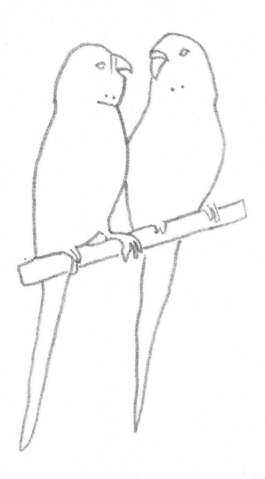

Draw Me Some Wings

My Cage

My cage is very important as this is where I'll spend the majority of my time. It will keep me safe and give me a home of my own.

When buying my cage you'll be able to see lots of them at the pet store to make your decision. Try to get me the very biggest cage you can. You'll have to take into account the space that you have at home where my cage will be sitting. You might also want to be able to move my cage from different locations. So you'll want to get one that you can handle and transport easily. Some people like to get two cages, one for my main home and a small cage or crate for taking me to the veterinarian, a short car ride, taking me outside or for taking me back to the pet store to pick out a new tasty treat. I really like the idea of going to get another treat with you.

The small cage or crate can also be used to put me in while you are giving my big main cage a thorough cleaning. This will keep me from flying away and getting lost or hurt.

Wire cages are best for me. I need ventilation, which is the airflow coming through my cage. Glass aquariums don't easily allow this. I also love to climb, so the bars on the wire cage can let me do that. Exercise is good for me just as it is for you. I am very active and like lots to do.

Do not set my cage in direct sunlight that is coming through a window. This can make my cage too hot for me. I like the temperature between 68 and 72 degrees. Also make sure that the air conditioner, fans or the heater are not constantly blowing on me. Keep my cage away from drafts too.

Be careful what you set my cage next to, or put on top of my cage. If I am too close to your curtains, cords, plants, books or other objects, I just might try to pull those into my cage and chew them to pieces. I'm sure you don't want to tell your teacher that your parakeet ate your homework.

While you are at the pet store, you'll see lots of different things that you can use to set up my cage for me to live in. I'll definitely need something for my water. Small dishes work fine for food, but I'll kick my food into an open water dish and make it undrinkable. I have also been known to turn my dish over and spill the water all over my cage and that makes a soggy mess. This is very uncomfortable for me to sit in, plus I'll get thirsty from having no water to drink. So you'll be better off getting me a water cup made especially for birds for drinking. This will attach right on my cage and keep my water clean and drinkable. Be sure to change my water daily. Besides clean water, I like it fresh too.

Most bird cages come with the food and water dishes. Food dishes that attach to the bars of the cage are better than an open dish that sits on the floor of my cage. Open dishes will get soiled from my waste when I use the bathroom.

I will also need a cage cover to put over the whole cage at night when it is time to sleep. This gives me a cozy feeling and wards off any drafts.

I will need some nice wooden perches too. Some of these perches come covered with sand paper. This sand paper will help keep my toenails filed down. I will chew on the sand paper too, so if you see it getting pretty ragged, take it out and throw it away and replace it with a nice fresh new one.

Keep my perches dry and clean. If you need to wash them, be sure they are totally dry before putting them back in my cage. Wet perches will cause me to have foot problems.

A nice swing in the cage would be so much fun. I love to climb and hop from branch to branch. My beak will help me grab the wire on my cage and assist me in my playful antics.

Parakeets love to chirp and kiss themselves in a mirror. You will laugh when you see how cute I am when I do this. I am very entertaining.

Be sure to clean my cage often. Don't use any bleach or harsh chemicals to clean my cage. These can cause respiratory problems for me. Check with the pet store for cleaners that are safe to use on my cage.

Setting up a cleaning schedule will help ensure that my home is clean and pleasant for me and for you. No one likes to live in a dirty, smelly home. Be sure my cage is totally dry before putting me back in.

Healthy Foods For Parakeets

It's not too hard to keep me happy and healthy if you feed me a good quality bird food and make my diet as varied as possible with healthy foods. This way I'll get a complete and balanced diet.

Bird seed will make up my main diet.

However, some fresh fruits and vegetables will make my days more fun by eating different foods.

Be sure the fruits and vegetables have been washed well to get off any bug sprays that may have been used when they were being grown.

Always feed me fresh food. Don't give me any foods that are starting to spoil or that are moldy. Moldy food will make me sick.

You can also find some special treats at the pet store that are made especially for me. These will add variety to my diet as well.

I would love a spray millet treat to peck at and eat the seeds. You just hang this right in my cage and I'll take care of the eating of it. You'll find these at your pet store too.

Parakeets also need grit to help grind our food, which will help to digest the food I eat. You do remember I have no teeth?

Be sure that my seed cup is full of actual seeds and not just the empty hulls from the seeds. I sometimes will drop the empty hulls back in the seed cup and it may look full, but it is not. Gently blow on the empty hulls to make them fall out of the seed cup. If my cup is actually empty, then refill it with fresh seeds for me.

You can offer me small amounts of fruits and vegetables every day. I might like these as a special treat.

Apples
Bananas
Berries
Cantaloupe

Watermelon
Grapes
Apricots (no pits)
Peas
Carrots
Squash (no seeds)

Remember, only give me small pieces of these, even if I beg for more.

If I don't eat all of the fresh treats that you give me after about an hour or so, take them out and throw them away. If you leave them in my cage, they will spoil, stink and cause ants or other bugs to come into my cage to get them.

Sometimes when trying a new food, it may take me awhile to get accustomed to the taste. So even if I refuse to eat it one day, the next day it could become my favorite treat.

Also, be sure that my bird seed is not dusty. As that will make me get asthma, from breathing in the dust.

Just talking about all this food is making me hungry.

What Foods Not To Feed Your Parakeet

These foods are not very good for me. These can make me sick and cause me to get diarrhea.

Iceberg lettuce
Rhubarb
Turnip greens
Beet tops
Parsley
Spinach
Avocado
Peach pits
Apple seeds
Cherry pits
Chocolate
Caffeine
Soda pop
Cheese
Milk
Alcohol

Vitamins & Minerals

If you are feeding me a good well-balanced diet, I may not need any extra vitamins and minerals unless I have been sick for some reason.

If I have been ill, your veterinarian will instruct you on how to give me any extra vitamins or minerals to make me better.

Never feed me your vitamins. Those are for people and they could make me very sick.

I know you are aware that I do need fresh water everyday and I appreciate you taking care of that for me.

Questions and Answers on Food

Here are a few questions for you to answer on what foods to feed me and what foods I should not eat.

What foods will make up my main diet? _____

Are fresh fruits and vegetables good for me? _____

Can I eat moldy food? _____

Should I have soda pop? _____

Chocolate sure smells good. Can I eat chocolate? _____

Can you name a food that is not good for me? _____

I hope you got these questions correct.

Food is an important part of my day. Eating the correct foods will keep me happy and healthy. I know you are in charge of feeding me correctly.

Color These Four Parakeets

Toys

You know that toys are fun.

I also need toys to keep me occupied and keep me from being bored.

Besides eating, playing is my most favorite thing to do.

You'll find plenty of toys at the pet store that I'll love. You can find small ones that I can grab with my beak and toss around. I love to climb. Ladders are a natural for me and I would really enjoy one or two.

I like to push things too. You'll find many good toys at the pet store. Check them over to be sure they are made well. Don't put really small toys in for me to play with, just in case I should swallow one.

Keep an eye on the condition of my toys. Some I can eat totally, which is fine if they are made for that. However, if some are made of plastic and I have really chewed them to the point of eating them, you may want to toss those in the trash.

If you have a special toy box for me, you can switch out my toys so that I only have two or three to play with at a time. This makes my days fun and I won't just be bored sitting in my cage. New toys keeps my little mind active and are fun to play with.

Playing is also good for me. It gives me exercise which is healthy for me, just as it is for you.

When my toys get dirty, take care to wash them. Don't use harsh chemicals on them, check at the pet store for a soap that is safe for me. Let my toys dry before putting them back in my toy box.

I would love to play with you and my toys everyday. You can laugh at my antics and watch how funny I am.

Mirrors are not just so I can look at how cute I am. They really let me chatter up a storm at my image in the mirror. I'll push and peck at the mirror, and entertain you and your friends.

Grooming Your Parakeet

Oh, I like being clean. You'll see me primping and preening my feathers all the time.

If you keep my cage and perches clean, I may not need a bath, but I may really enjoy one. Sometimes baths are just for fun. Especially if it is warm outside. You can buy me a little bathtub at the pet store. Some of the bath tubs even have a mirror on the bottom, which is fun to watch me swish and splash in.

You won't need to do much to encourage me to get in the water. Just be patient and I'll normally do all the work myself. Your job is to be sure I do not get in the way of any drafts or air conditioners or fans blowing on me when I am trying to dry off. Be sure to give me a bath early in the day, so that I have plenty of time to dry off before bedtime.

If I just won't take a bath, and you feel I need to get cleaned, you can find some special bird bath sprays at the pet store.

You can keep a good eye out to see if any of my toenails might need to be trimmed. If they do, you can get a special toenail clippers at the pet store that are designed for pets. Have an expert show you how to trim my nails. You do not want to cut into the quick in my toes. This will hurt me and cause my toe to bleed. You can buy some medicine at the pet store to help stop the bleeding, but it is better if you just not cut my toenails that short.

Sometimes we will get mites. These are little bugs that are on my body. If I appear to really be biting at my body, check me over for mites. Or take me to your veterinarian for a proper diagnosis. You'll be able to get some medicine from the pet store or your vet to treat me, my cage and my perches if I do get any mites.

My beak rarely gives me any trouble if you give me items to chew on and rub my beak on. If my beak does get over grown, you'll need to take me to the veterinarian so my beak can be clipped down.

You can make me a little grooming kit, and keep all my supplies together and only use them on me.

My Feathers

There comes a time when you might want to clip my wings in order to tame me down, so I don't fly away from you.

Some people think this is a bad idea, and especially bad if you don't do it correctly.

Taming me to your finger or hand can be done while I am safely in my cage. Once I get used to you and getting on and off your finger while in my cage, you can slowly bring your hand out of the cage with me on it. Sometimes just gently holding one of my toes with your finger will keep me steady and will help keep me from flying away. Practice holding my toe with your finger while I am in my cage. Then I won't be surprised when you do this, once I am out of my cage.

If you take me into a small room to tame me down, you'll be able to catch me easier than if I am flying all over the house. Go slow with me, and soon I'll be sitting on your finger or your shoulders.

Trimming my flight feathers should be done by an experienced bird person or veterinarian. My feathers will grow back, and once I am tame you won't need to trim them again.

I will also go through a moult. Moult is where I will lose some feathers. This may happen about once a year. You'll see a few of my feathers in my cage, which is normal. If my feathers are falling out to the point of you seeing bald spots on me, take me to your veterinarian to see what is ailing me, and to get me back on track to being healthy.

If you see me just pulling and plucking my feathers, it could be caused from nervousness. Check to be sure another animal is not pestering me, even through the bars of my cage. Be sure any noises are not too loud or too close to me and my cage. I also need a good nights sleep, so keep things dark and quiet at night and cover my cage. Sometimes feather plucking is caused by just being bored.

My Beak

My beak is quite impressive. Even though I have no teeth, my beak can still put a painful bite on you if you scare me or you are mean to me. I may also bite if I am in pain.

My beak should never be allowed to get overgrown. You will want to purchase a cuttlebone from the pet store. Cuttlebones have calcium in them, important salts and minerals and will help to keep my beak trim.

If my beak does get overgrown, you'll need to take me to the veterinarian to get it clipped down. You can avoid this by being sure I have plenty of things to play with and grab, all the while keeping my beak in good shape.

My beak also helps me move around my cage. I like to grab the bars with my beak and rub it on my perches and my swings.

You might even see that I have a little tongue in my beak too.

You'll notice a hard substance on the top portion of my beak. This is called a cere. This will change colors as I grow older. If I am a male parakeet, this cere will turn blue when I am about 3 to 4 months old. If I am a female parakeet, the cere will turn white and then to tan when I am about 10 to 12 months old. You'll notice my two little nostrils showing on the cere.

Teaching Your Parakeet To Talk

Oh what fun this is going to be.

Teaching me to talk will take time, repetition and patience.

Only attempt to teach me one word at a time. You will need to say this word to me over and over. Every time you come by my cage, say the word to me. Repeat the word for about 10 minutes straight. When you cover me up at night, repeat the word to me too.

Don't have more than one person try to teach me the word. Different pitches of voices will make it harder for me to learn.

You will notice that once I start to say the first word, the next word you teach me will come quicker.

I can also learn to whistle like you. Keep practicing with me. I'll soon surprise you one day, and oh how proud you'll be.

Taking Your Parakeet Outdoors

Taking me outdoors to get some fresh air when the weather is nice can be a lot of fun.

You'll know I'm happy by all the singing and chirping I am doing.

Here are some tips to keep me safe.

Be sure that my door is securely latched. Maybe you'll want to add an extra clamp on the door.

Be sure that I am not sitting directly in the sun. I should have a nice shady spot within my cage, so I don't get too hot. You may need to tie a towel on a portion of my cage, to give me some shade.

Hang my cage out of the reach of other pets and wild animals that may be in the area.

Be sure that I have some fresh cool water.

If I can fly, don't trust that I'll stay on your shoulder. I may fly away and not find my way back. You may never see me again.

If you have cut my flight feathers off and I can't fly, this will make me an easy catch for any free roaming cats or other animals in the area.

My cage is the safest place for me when I am outside getting some fresh air and sunshine.

It is best to stay outside with me. Then if any danger comes along you can take me back indoors. You'll also be able to see if the weather starts to change and a storm comes along.

You can take me outdoors as often as the weather is nice. I will never get bored of this.

Parakeet Maze

Parakeets like seeds. Can you take a red crayon and help this hungry parakeet find the seeds through the maze? Then will you take an orange crayon and help him find the cuttle bone?

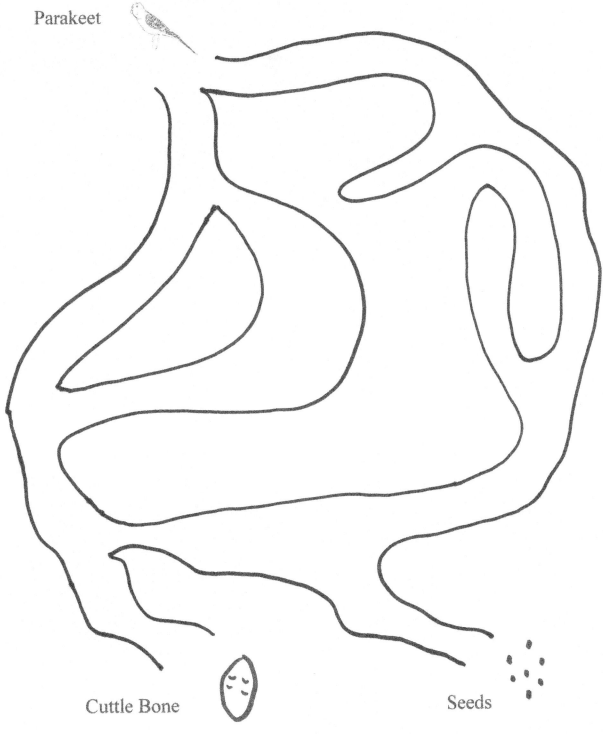

Color Us

Health Issues for Parakeets

Parakeets can have a few health problems. You'll soon learn from my day to day activity if I am not feeling well.

Normally I am cheerful and wanting to play with my toys, look at myself in the mirror and climb on the bars of my cage.

If you see me sitting listless, or sitting with my head under my wing, and won't move, even if you come over to my cage, something may be wrong with me.

These are some of the health issues I can get.

I can get pneumonia.

I can get diarrhea or constipated.

I can get lice or mites.

I can catch a cold.

I can injure myself while in or outside of my cage. Sometimes my injuries don't show up for a few hours.

I can get sick from eating bad or moldy food.

I can get heat stroke. Be sure my cage is not sitting in the hot sun.

When in doubt about my health, talk to a bird expert or a veterinarian.

With the proper care, I'll be back to my cheerful happy self.

Missing Vowels

Here are more puzzles that you can do. Fill in the missing vowels from the words below. Some of the words pertain to what parakeets like to eat and do, and the last two words are what your parakeet should have plenty of when he is outside.

Use these vowels: A – E – I – O – U - Y

P _ R _ K _ _ T S

F _ _ T H _ R S

S _ _ D S

F L _

B _ _ K

P _ R C H

C H _ R P

S W _ N G

C L _ M B

W _ N G S

S _ N G

S H _ D _

W _ T _ R

Word Find

Below is a word find puzzle. Can you find the following words in the puzzle? Circle the words and check them off the list when you find them.

___ PARAKEET

___ CAGE

___ FEATHER

___ TAIL

___ CLAWS

___ BEAK

___ SUNSHINE

___ SHADE

___ SWING

___ WATER

___ COLOR

___ FOOD

B	N	D	V	F	O	O	D	R	P	F	A	S	M	S	W	I	N	G	Z
M	H	S	R	A	C	B	I	T	S	B	F	U	R	A	W	A	T	R	E
U	S	A	A	G	H	J	U	M	P	E	E	N	C	T	A	M	S	A	Q
F	E	A	T	H	E	R	R	U	P	V	A	S	S	T	T	W	A	T	C
I	E	M	P	P	L	E	M	H	O	V	S	H	A	D	E	E	H	O	A
C	D	O	X	I	O	P	R	R	A	C	C	I	A	S	R	J	H	N	G
O	A	N	S	J	E	R	T	Y	U	B	I	N	N	Y	B	A	B	G	E
B	H	O	P	V	B	V	C	A	E	A	S	E	R	S	U	N	N	U	R
E	I	T	N	T	G	H	K	A	C	A	R	R	B	Y	W	R	X	E	O
A	J	U	P	P	Y	O	L	O	V	U	W	A	T	A	I	L	S	I	N
K	C	L	A	W	S	R	B	E	C	P	A	R	A	K	E	E	T	O	N

Color Me

Daily Care Chart

Below is a chart to help you remember to take care of your pet parakeet.

You may want to make some copies of the chart, before you start to use it. Then you'll have plenty for the year and you can hang it someplace where you'll see it to remind you about my daily care.

Put a little smiley face, star or check mark each time you have taken care of my needs.

Keeping me properly fed and clean will make me happy and healthy.

Be sure to clean the area outside of my cage too. Just in case I've kicked some waste or food out. This will prevent ants and other bugs from coming, and help to control any odors.

	Sunday	Monday	Tuesday	Wednesday	Thursday	Friday	Saturday
Feeding							
Watering							
Playtime							
Clean Daily							
Clean Weekly							

Make Your Own Note Cards

On the next page you will find two different pictures for you to make your own note cards.

Carefully tear the page out of your book. Cut on the dotted line and trim the edge that was torn out of your book.

Fold the paper in half.

Color the pictures and add any flowers, trees, clouds, the sun, etc.

Add your own wording on the inside, such as, Happy Birthday, Get Well Soon or whatever else you'd like.

Give the note card to someone special.

Made For You By:

Made For You By:

Make Your Own Bookmark

Below are three bookmarks. Cut out and draw your own Parakeet on one end and color them in nice bright colors for your books. If you cover them with clear mailing tape, it will make them sturdy.

I Love My Parakeet!

I Love My Parakeet!

I Love My Parakeet!

After you cut out your bookmarks, draw or write your name on the back sides before covering them with tape.

Other Books in the Series

When you need other animal care books with fun activities, ask for these books from your favorite bookseller.

Title	ISBN
I Want A Pet Chinchilla	ISBN: 978-1491274415
I Want A Pet Hamster	ISBN: 978-1491274286
I Want A Pet Rabbit	ISBN: 978-1491273630
I Want A Pet Guinea Pig	ISBN: 978-1491273968
I Want A Pet Ferret	ISBN: 978-1491274118
I Want A Pet Rat	ISBN: 978-1491274224
I Want A Pet Tortoise	ISBN: 978-1492303275
I Want A Pet Turtle	ISBN: 978-1492303312
I Want A Pet Parakeet	ISBN: 978-1492303350
I Want A Pet Parrot	ISBN: 978-1492303398
I Want A Pet Cockatiel	ISBN: 978-1492303435
I Want A Pet Iguana	ISBN: 978-1492303473
I Want A Pet Bearded Dragon	ISBN: 978-1492303541
I Want A Pet Chameleon	ISBN: 978-1492303633
I Want A Pet Gecko	ISBN: 978-1492303701
I Want A Pet Lizard	ISBN: 978-1492303732
I Want A Pet Snake	ISBN: 978-1492303800
I Want A Pet Betta	ISBN: 978-1492303855
I Want A Kitten	ISBN: 978-1492303886
I Want A Puppy	ISBN: 978-1492303916
I Want A Pony	ISBN: 978-1492303954

Made in the USA
Las Vegas, NV
16 April 2024

88737448R00031